How to Stay Safe at Home and On-line

Ira Wood

The Rosen Publishing Group's

READING ROOM
Collection™

New York

Published in 2002 by The Rosen Publishing Group, Inc.
29 East 21st Street, New York, NY 10010

First Library Edition 2002

Book Design: Ron A. Churley

Photo Credits: Cover, p. 1 © Bob Daemmrich/The Image Works; p. 4 by Donna M. Scholl; p. 7 © Ron Chapple/FPG International; pp. 8, 11, 12, 15, 16, 19 © Seth Dinnerman; p. 20 © Johnny Crawford/The Image Works.

Library of Congress Cataloging-in-Publication Data

Wood, Ira, 1972-
  How to stay safe at home and on-line / Ira Wood.
      p. cm.
Summary: Provides important safety tips regarding being home alone and being online.
  ISBN 0-8239-3722-4
  1. Safety education—Juvenile literature. 2. Children and strangers—Juvenile literature. 3. Child abuse—Prevention—Juvenile literature. 4. Internet and children—Safety measures—Juvenile literature. [1. Safety.] I. Title.
  HQ770.7 .W66 2002
  613.6'071—dc21
                                        2001006836

Manufactured in the United States of America

For More Information
Kids Com: Play Smart, Stay Safe, Have Fun
http://www.kidscom.com

Contents

Safety First

Home is where you should feel safe and **secure**. What if you are home alone and someone you don't know knocks on the door? What if you are **on-line** and someone you don't know tries to talk to you? Sometimes bad people try to meet you this way. It is important to know how to be safe when you are home alone or on-line.

Staying safe is easy when you know what to do.

You Have an Important Job

When you are home alone, you are **in charge** of keeping yourself safe. A big part of being home alone is knowing you should never open the door to a **stranger**. Don't let anyone know that you are home alone. Work out a plan with your mom or dad that will keep you in charge and help you stay safe.

You and your parent should talk about how you can stay safe when you are home alone.

Be Smart

If the doorbell rings when you are home alone, don't open the door. Don't worry about missing a visitor who comes to the door. If it's important, that person can come back when your mom or dad is home. If the person won't go away, call a neighbor your family trusts. If the neighbor isn't home, call **911**. If someone calls on the phone, say that Mom or Dad is in the shower or taking a nap.

Keep the door closed and locked even if you think the person at the door has left.

9

Should You Let Neighbors In?

Will your parents be angry with you for not letting your neighbor in when you are home alone? No way! You won't get in trouble. You could put yourself in danger if you let the wrong person into your house. Talk to your mom or dad about it. Ask which neighbors and friends are safe and which ones are not.

If your door has a peephole, you should look through it to see who is knocking before you open the door.

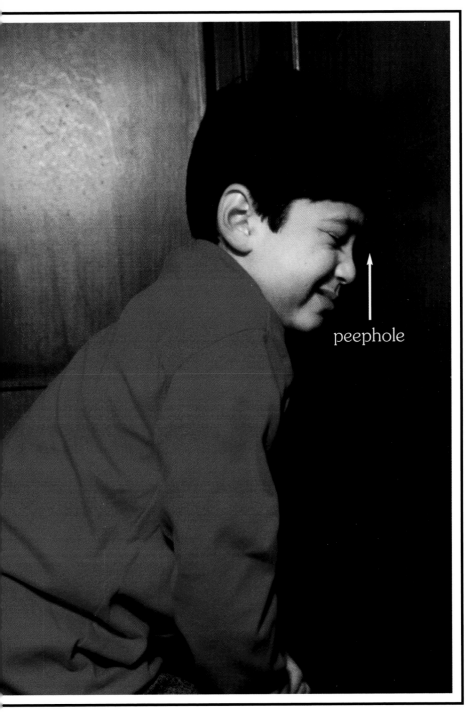

peephole

The Right Thing to Do

A woman you don't know comes to the door when you are home alone. She says she is a friend of your mom's and has a package for her. You don't let her into the house. Did you do the right thing? You bet you did! Even though the woman was your mom's friend, you made the safe choice. Your mom's friend can come back later. A good person will understand and **respect** that you are trying to stay safe.

Don't open the door for anyone you don't know.

13

Don't Be Fooled

Sometimes bad people do things we don't understand. A bad person may pretend to be a good person and trick you into trusting him or her. Some people may even pretend to be police officers. If someone comes to the door and says he or she is a police officer, don't open the door. Ask the officer to come back later. If the person doesn't leave, call 911. It's always better to be safe.

A real police officer will understand why you may call 911 before opening the door.

On-line Liars

Some people may tell lies on-line using the **Internet** or e-mail. When you are typing messages on your computer to another person, you don't always know who is at the other end. A person who says she is a girl named Judy could really be a boy named Joe. Don't give your last name, address, or phone number to anyone on-line. Make sure a grown-up knows when you are using the computer.

Being on-line can be fun, but you should make sure it's safe, too.

Strangers On-line

While searching the Internet for help with your homework, you see an ad that says, "Make Friends! Have Fun!" You decide to check it out. Someone named Ray asks you how old you are and where you live. These questions make you feel **uncomfortable**. What should you do? Don't respond to this person, and tell your mom or dad right away. Always let your parents know when you are on-line.

Having your mom or dad around when you try new things on-line is the safe and smart thing to do.

On-line Dangers

Some people go on-line just to trick other people. Sometimes the people they want to trick are kids. A bad person may ask you questions that make you feel uncomfortable. Never tell people you meet on-line your address, and never agree to meet them somewhere. If a person says something on-line that gives you a bad feeling, don't reply. Tell your parents right away.

Most people you meet on-line are friendly, but it is a good idea to watch out for people who might want to trick you.

21

Stay Safe

Did someone on-line ask you a lot of questions? Did a neighbor try to make you open the door for him or her when you were home alone? These things may never happen to you, but now you know what you can do to keep yourself safe. You also know that you should tell your parents about anything that makes you feel uncomfortable. Be smart and stay safe!

Glossary

in charge   Being in control.

Internet   A worldwide computer
                       system a person can
                       use to get facts and
                       talk with others.

911   A phone number that
                       is used to reach the fire
                       department or police
                       station quickly.

on-line   Connected to a
                       computer system.

respect   To think highly of
                       someone.

secure   Free from harm.

stranger   Someone you do not
                       know.

uncomfortable   Feeling scared and
                       unsure of yourself or
                       something around you.

Index

E
e-mail, 17

F
friend(s), 10, 13, 18

I
Internet, 17, 18

N
neighbor(s), 9, 10, 22

O
on-line, 5, 17, 21, 22

P
parents, 10, 18, 21, 22
plan, 6

R
respect, 13

S
stranger, 6

U
uncomfortable, 18, 21, 22

V
visitor, 9